The Silent God

Why God Does Not Speak

Jeffrey D. Johnson

Wipf & Stock
PUBLISHERS
Eugene, Oregon

Wipf and Stock Publishers
199 W 8th Ave, Suite 3
Eugene, OR 97401

The Silent God
Why God Does Not Speak
By Johnson, Jeffrey D.

ISBN 13: 978-1-55635-077-1
ISBN 10: 1-55635-077-5
Publication date 11/30/2006

About Israel Today Ministries

Three-fold Purpose:

- Teach the Church about Israel
- Teach Israel about their Messiah
- Help feed those in need (Romans 15:27; Genesis 12:1-3)

To receive Dr. Johnson's "teaching letters," or, if you would like to send a gift to Israel Today Ministries, or if you would like Dr. Johnson to speak at your church event, school, or small group, contact:

Israel Today Ministries
P.O. Box 150288
Arlington, TX 76015
Phone/Fax 817.468.4441
E mail: Galileeman@juno.com

This is Yossef (Joseph) and Abigail. Your monthly donations help feed little ones like these.

"Inasmuch as ye have done it unto one of the least of these my brethren, ye have done it unto me" –Jesus, Matthew 25:40

About Dr. Jeffrey D. Johnson

- Three decades in ministry
- Founder / Director of Israel Today Ministries
- Director of tours to the Middle East
- Senior pastor in Ohio, Massachusetts and California
- Almost 7 years directorship with International Ministries to Israel (formerly, The American Association for Jewish Evangelism, where the famed Hyman Appelman was the first president)
- Conference speaker
- Bible expositor
- Guest lecturer
- Author

Born and raised in the Midwest, Dr. Johnson took his B.D. from Massillon Baptist College, his MA from Moody Bible Institute, and his Th.M. and Th.D. from Christian Bible College. His passion for Israel, the Jewish roots of Christianity and Bible prophecy, is well known. His teaching will stir your heart to follow the Lord and to love and *"pray for the peace of Jerusalem"* (Psalm 122:6).

As an "Itinerant Bible Teacher," Dr. Johnson will travel anywhere to proclaim God's redeeming Grace through our Lord and Savior Jesus the Messiah, *"to the Jew first, and also to the Greek"* (Romans 1:16).

His call is to *"Teach the Church about Israel; Teach Israel about their Messiah; and to feed those in need"* (Genesis 12:3; Romans 15:27).

Dr. Jeff and his wife, Louise, have purposed to serve the Lord trusting God to provide the funds and resources for their livelihood.

Israel Today Ministries, founded by Dr. Johnson, is a faith ministry, supported by "love offerings" from those desiring to bless Israel. Dr. Jeff and Louise have been commissioned and sent out by their home church.

Comments from Christian Leaders

I am pleased to recommend him to churches as an able expositor of the Word of God.

– *the late* **John Walvoord**, Chancellor,
Dallas Theological Seminary

A Bible Expositor with special insights on the origin, nature and destiny of God's chosen people, Israel.

– **John C. Whitcomb**, Bible Scholar, Author, Professor

A careful expositor of Scripture.

– **Homer Kent**, President Emeritus,
Grace College and Seminary

A practitioner of all that he preaches.

– **Paige Patterson**, former President of the
Southern Baptist Convention, President,
Southeastern Baptist Theological Seminary

He has a wonderful grasp of Jewish history and liturgy.

– **Edgar C. James**, Professor, Moody Bible Institute

He is a person who has been uniquely prepared by God to preach and teach about God's special people. Any one who hears him will come away with a great love for the people of Abraham.

–**Dick Dahlquist**, Chair, Pastoral Studies, Acting Dean,
Grace College of Graduate Studies

He has a gifted teaching ministry which encompasses Biblical prophecy and insights into modern-day Judaism.

–the late **Paul Tassell**, Bible Scholar, Author,
former National Representative of the G.A.R.B.C.

He has a great ministry.

– **LaVerne Butler**, former President of Mid-Continent Baptist College, Scholar, Conference Speaker, President, Pulpit Aflame

Your heart will be thrilled as he ministers the prophetic Scriptures.

– the late **Alden A. Gannett**, President Emeritus of Southeastern Bible College, Bible Scholar, Author, Conference Speaker, President, Gannett Ministries

He loves the people and nation of Israel. He has given himself to a thorough study of God's ancient people and of the prophetic.

– **Ivan H. French**, Pastor Emeritus, Pleasant View Bible Church, former Professor, Grace College and Seminary

Why God Does Not Speak

"Lord, where are you? I cried out to you over and over again. You have been silent! Where are you?"

Christians may face the challenge of God's silence. You know, when the illness comes; financial difficulty; relational problems; emotional challenges; spiritual depression; temptation. Where is God? Why is He silent? All believers in Jesus will face tests and trials somewhere along their journey.

Where is God? Do you find, at times, when you cry out to Him He is silent? I have.

When God reveals Himself it is purely an act of grace through His Spirit. It isn't that God is silent, it is however, that He chooses to reveal Himself to His children at specific times. When He does reveal His purpose in your life it is usually very clear, and sometimes suddenly.

Consider God appearing to **Moses** in the burning bush. It wasn't until Moses experienced an incredible season of trial and testing that God revealed His purpose (Exodus 3).

Look at **Elijah** after his victory on the mountain. He was exhausted and depressed ready to die and suddenly an angel touched him (1 Kings 19).

During a time of mourning **Isaiah** was in the Temple and the Lord was revealed to him. His purpose was made clear. His path was set in motion. He now had clear direction and understanding of his circumstances (Isaiah 6).

It was during a time of civil and political upheaval that young **Jeremiah** heard from God. God assured him that he was on this earth, this time, during this occasion for a purpose. Jeremiah was set in motion once he understood from God why the times were they way they were. It now made sense to this weeping prophet (Jeremiah 1).

Ruth suffered the death of her husband and experienced great loss. She found God in the process and yet still suffered hardship until the Lord replenished her life with blessing (Ruth 1:16; 4:10-14).

Esther found that she was brought into the kingdom for such a time as this. What was this special time? It was a time of political turmoil in which the Jews would face extermination unless someone intervened. She found out that God orchestrated events in order to bring about something greater than herself. It wasn't an easy task before her. In fact her life could have been taken from her if she failed. She prayed and asked others to pray. It worked, God answered (Esther 4).

The priest **Zacharias** going about his daily duties of the Temple was troubled when he finally heard from God. He and his wife were both righteous before Lord. They loved

God and yet they had a test in their lives. Their burden, Elizabeth was barren, a curse in that culture. So they prayed and prayed to God. He was silent for so long and then suddenly God spoke through the angel Gabriel.

It startled Zacharias. In fact, he did not believe that God was answering his prayers. After all it has been so long. Why now? He wasn't sure what to make of it all (Luke 1).

At the **Pool of Bethesda** there was a man with an infirmity desiring to be healed. He had this infirmity for 38 years. For almost 4 decades he suffered. He prayed and waited, prayed and waited. Then Jesus saw him. For almost 40 years there was silence. Then God appeared in the flesh (John 5).

Stephen, a man of faith, Spirit filled, was living out his faith. He was put to death for his belief in Jesus. It wasn't until moments before he passed into the eternal that he saw Jesus and understood that he was in the perfect will of God, standing true to the faith (Acts 7).

Beloved, do you see a pattern here? Being a Christian, being a follower of God does not mean that you will be trouble free. In every case, the believer experienced obstacles and valleys and sometimes it cost them their lives. Months, years, decades, then God speaks and it is then clear regarding the question, "Why?"

It seems to me that the propensity of God is to be silent. It is an act of grace and love. His silence strengthens our faith. *"Faith is the substance of things hoped form, the evidence of things not seen (Hebrews 11:1).*

Is God there? Yes! He is Emmanuel, God with us. You can see Him in the sidereal universe (Psalm 19:1). You can see Him in the gift of children (Luke 18:15-17). He is there in every breath you take (Acts 17:25). Every changed life is testimonial to the fact that God is there (2 Corinthians 5:17). Every miracle points us to God (Luke 1:37).

Sometimes we cannot see because our hearts are not clean. When we humble our hearts before Him and seek Him and confess our sin He will cleanse our hearts and we will see Him (Hebrews 12:14; 1 John 1:8-10). To seek the path of peace, holiness and love is a difficult road. It is not natural for human beings to do so. It is only through His spirit seeking to follow His Christ shall we see God, for Christ is God (1 John 4:4; Hebrews 11:6).

- Therefore beloved, when God is silent, remember He **IS** there. He promised He will never leave nor forsake us (Hebrews 13:5).

- When God is silent, it is an act of grace and love to strengthen our faith (Hebrews 11:1).

- When God is silent, He has a greater purpose in mind, though we may not fully understand (Romans 8:28-39).

- When God is silent, the Spirit will make intercession for us, for we do not know what to pray (Romans 8:26, 27).

- When God is silent, we are to wait and hope for that which we do not see, nor understand (Romans 8:24, 25; Isaiah 40:31)

- When God is silent, do not despair, for at the exact moment, when the time is right, He will speak, and you will know what it means to seek Him.

"Shall not the Judge of all the earth do right?" (Genesis 18:25)

"Blessed be the Lord God of Israel for ever and ever. And all the people said, Amen, and praised the Lord." (1Chronicles 16:36)